THAT'S SUN!

Judy Kentor Schmauss

Contents

Rigby®

A Harcourt Achieve Imprint

www.Rigby.com
1-800-531-5015

What would happen if the sun did not exist? The earth would be a cold, dark place. Did you know that trees, plants, animals, and humans all depend on the sun for heat, light, food, and air?

This is the Inca's Temple of the Sun in Cuzco, Peru.

Almost every ancient culture had some kind of myth that related to the sun. Even people thousands of years ago understood how important the sun is to all living things. In this book, we'll look at what the sun is and why it is so important in our lives.

What is the sun?

Did you know that the sun is actually a star? It is similar to other stars that you see in the sky. In fact, the sun is one of at least four hundred billion stars in the Milky Way galaxy.

Stars come in different shapes and sizes. There are names for each type of star. Our sun is a medium star known as a *Yellow Dwarf*.

sun

Milky Way galaxy

What is the sun made of?

The sun is not a solid object. It is made up of different gases. These gases are always moving around and mixing together.

Hydrogen makes up the largest portion of gas in the sun. Helium is another gas found in the sun. It's the same gas that makes a balloon float up in the air. The rest of the sun is made up of smaller amounts of other gases.

The sun is made up of layers. The core is the very center layer. That's where the gases mix with each other and make heat. It's the hottest part of the star. The energy made in the core travels outward through the radiation zone, the second layer of the sun.

In the next layer, the convection zone, the energy moves around in large cells, gaining strength as it moves outward. The photosphere is the fourth layer of the sun. It's the edge you see around the sun when you look at it.

radiation zone

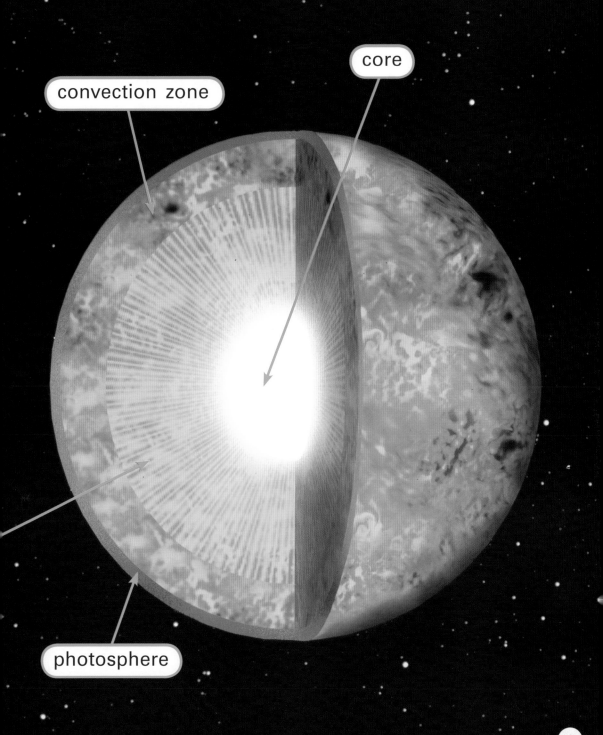

convection zone

core

photosphere

Outside of the photosphere is the chromosphere. That's where the heat escapes. The corona is the very outside layer. It is what we see in pictures that look like flames shooting out from the sun.

corona

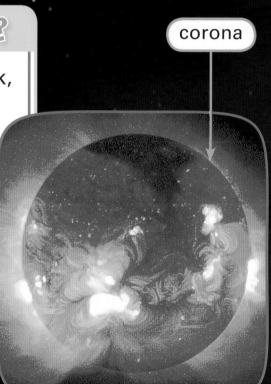

How big is the sun?

The diameter of the sun is 870,000 miles wide. In other words, it would take about 109 Earths lined up next to each other to stretch across the sun. It would take over 1.3 million Earths to fill the space taken up by the sun.

Earth

sun

99° Fahrenheit

451° Fahrenheit

How hot is the sun?

Let's say that it's a hot summer day, and you're sweating. The temperature outside might be about 99 degrees Fahrenheit. That's pretty hot! Now think about this. Inside the sun's core, it's 27 million degrees Fahrenheit! Does that make you feel cooler?

Did You Know?

Lightning is even hotter than the sun!

How far away is the sun?

If you walk to school, you probably have no more than about 2 miles to go. Compare that to how far the sun is from Earth—about 93 million miles away! But compared to other stars, the sun is close to us. Other stars are more than 6 trillion miles away from Earth. That's why the sun looks so much bigger than other stars.

You are here.

93 million miles

How does the sun affect our lives?

We have depended on the sun for millions of years. The sun heats the air, the land, and the ocean. When the ocean water gets warm, some of it evaporates, or changes, into vapor, or steam. When the vapor cools, we get rain or snow.

The rain or snow then drops down to the ground. This process provides water for plants, humans, and animals.

The plants use the water and the sun's light to complete the process of **photosynthesis**. During this process, plants take in **carbon dioxide** (CO_2) in the air, using it to make food. Then the plants give off oxygen. Humans and animals breathe in the oxygen and breathe out the carbon dioxide. The cycle keeps going around and around.

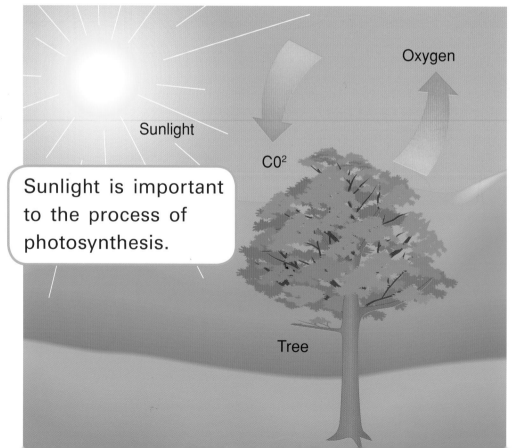

Oxygen

Sunlight

CO_2

Sunlight is important to the process of photosynthesis.

Tree

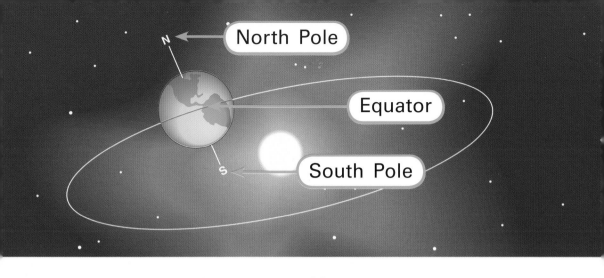

How does the sun affect how hot it is where I live?

The sun's rays shine the hottest at the earth's **equator**. At the very top of the earth is the North Pole. At the very bottom of the earth is the South Pole. The closer you live to the equator, the warmer it is there.

Did You Know?

A lamp might give off up to 100 watts of light. The sun gives off 40,000 watts of light from every square inch of its surface.

How long will the sun continue to heat the earth?

Scientists believe that the sun has been giving off heat and light for over 4 billion years. They also believe it will keep giving heat and light for another 5 billion years or so. Someday it will burn itself out, much like other stars do.

The sun is just one of billions of stars found in the galaxy.

How do scientists study the sun?

Scientists are very careful when studying the sun. The heat of the sun's rays is so strong that it can cause blindness. That is why people should never stare at the sun, even with sunglasses on. There is no safe way to look at the sun through a normal telescope either.

Did You Know?

A special x-ray telescope was made to help scientists study the sun. This telescope was sent into space on a Japanese satellite. The satellite's name was *Yohkoh,* which means sunbeam.

What is solar energy?

Solar energy is energy from the sun that can be used to provide electricity. There are many ways that solar energy is collected and stored. Some homes use solar energy for heat.

Did You Know?

In just one hour, the earth gets enough sunlight to light the world for a year.

Solar cars use energy from the sun.

Some cars even run on solar energy. Panels on the tops of these cars collect the sun's energy and turn it into electricity. The batteries in these cars store energy from the sun, just like gas tanks store gasoline in gas-powered cars.

More uses for solar energy are being discovered every day. Maybe one day everything will be powered by the sun. Solar energy just might be the way we heat our homes and schools and run our computers and washing machines.

This solar power plant captures the sun and turns it into energy for people to use in their homes.

Glossary

carbon dioxide a colorless, odorless gas that is found in the atmosphere

equator the invisible line that divides the earth in half width-wise

photosynthesis the process by which plants make carbohydrates from carbon dioxide and water

Index